Creating Plays with Children

by SANDRA SANDERS

CITATION PRESS   NEW YORK   1970

Copyright © 1970 by Scholastic Magazines, Inc. All Rights reserved. This edition published by Citation Press, Professional Relations Division, Scholastic Magazines, Inc. Editorial office: 50 West 44th Street, New York, N. Y. 10036.

CONTENTS

Introduction	5
The Three Sillies	19
Hansel and Gretel	27
Tragedy in the Graveyard (Tom Sawyer)	38
The Wizard of Oz	45
Rip Van Winkle	64
Julius Caesar	79

DRAMATICS:
PEDAGOGY VS. REALITY

ONCE UPON A TIME, when children gave a play they would dress up like bunnies and carrots and line up in front of the P.T.A. Often they forgot their lines or couldn't be heard beyond the third row. But everyone was pleased, anyway.

Today, dramatics is thought of, in educational circles at least, as an activity for the classroom. There, children can *play* instead of *giving* plays — improvise scenes from favorite stories, and role-play or pantomime characters. They can become the lonely new boy in school, a cranky old lady, or a spoiled princess. They can act out anger or fear or surprise, and blow off steam. They have fun. And for a few minutes, they can step into the skin of another human being.

Classroom dramatics can be a release for children, whereas the old-time auditorium production inhibited them. Today, classroom dramatics is in. Auditorium programs are out.

Or are they?

As everybody knows, educational theory is one thing while practice is often another; and most teachers still have to prepare a program for the auditorium each year. After all, children do like to show off on stage; parents do want to see their children perform; and teachers — well the teachers sometimes enjoy it too.

But does the auditorium program have to be the same old rote and sing-song ordeal of former days? Isn't there some way to get around the stiffness and artificiality — a way to make an auditorium production creative and meaningful — a *real* experience in dramatics?

When I started teaching, the teacher in the room next door was an actress who substituted between roles. She invited my class to join hers for some role-playing and improvising. Before long, my fifth-graders wanted to act out every story they heard. At the time, I was reading *Tom Sawyer* to them, and they quickly made a play of it, almost by themselves. We put it on in the auditorium, and it was a huge success. After that, I never did a play any other way. There were all sorts of serendipitous benefits for the children. It was easier for them — and for me — than doing a printed play. The results were almost professional, since the children were *really* acting and not reciting. And best of all, it was a lot of fun.

Strictly speaking, "the method" is *to let the children make up their own play* based on a story they know well and like — one they have read together or one you have read to them.

To point the way toward child-oriented plays, I have included six sample plays — some of which have been created by children and some that I have worked out. I have also included some suggestions for using the techniques of classroom dramatics in putting on these or other printed plays.

With ingenuity, will, and a little bit of luck, dramatics — even in the auditorium — can be a creative and satisfying experience.

CHOOSING A STORY

Ideally, an auditorium program should develop spontaneously as your children act out their favorite stories. In real life, of course, what the teacher wants seldom happens spontaneously.

Most likely, the auditorium committee will trap you one day and remind you that it's your turn to do a program; and you will be forced to choose a story yourself and see to it that it becomes a play.

The story should have these two elements:
- both male and female characters; and
- *lots* of characters (or a crowd scene) since every child who wants to participate should have a part.

The simpler the plot the better, of course. Humorous books often have short scenes that work well. Children love slapstick; and when it comes to drama, they are partial to a little violence. In short, it's easier for them to act physically than vocally.

Fairy tales have two advantages: Most children already know them, and they often include crowds of peasants or members of a king's court.

Many fairy tales, unfortunately, require impossible

special effects such as growing a long nose or changing lead into gold. Children often find ingenious ways of getting around such difficulties; but plays usually work better when the teacher can picture beforehand how the story can be made into a play.

CHOOSING A SCENE

It all starts when the class reads a story together or when you read one to them. Reading aloud is an enjoyable experience for both the teacher and the children. No one is ever too old to be read to. Shared stories are as much fun for a sixth-grader as for a fourth-grader, for a child who reads well as for one who reads poorly. The reading should be leisurely and pleasant. If time is short, choose a short story, fairy tale, or legend. If you have plenty of time, read the class a good book — a chapter a day.

Afterward, ask which scenes the class liked best. With luck, they'll choose one you've already thought of as appropriate for the class to dramatize. This isn't as unlikely as it seems. Children like dramatic and funny scenes. But if they do pick a scene that is impossible for a play, point out the acting possibilities of one *you* feel is more workable.

ACTING OUT THE SCENE

The First Day: Retelling the Story . . .

Suppose the class has chosen the graveyard scene

from *Tom Sawyer*. You say, "Who'd like to tell what happened to Tom and Huck in the graveyard?" Someone will start telling the story. "Well, Tom and Huck are hiding behind this tree, and then they see a light coming." If the storyteller is leaving anything out, someone else will probably remind him: "You forgot why they were in the graveyard. Huck had this formula for getting rid of warts."

If the children do leave out something important, do some prompting of your own (leaving your own questions till the end, if possible, in order not to interrupt the flow). "How do you think Tom and Huck felt in the graveyard?" you may ask; and "Did Huck feel the way Tom did? Did he show it the same way?" The idea is to start the children thinking about the feelings of the characters and how they are shown.

In a few minutes, the class has retold the graveyard scene, and at least two good things have probably happened: they've reminded themselves of the scene's main elements, and they have unconsciously simplified it. (The murder scene in *Tom Sawyer* is much more complex than it became when the fifth-graders who wrote the play on p. 43 reconstructed it.)

. . . and Acting It Out

Now comes the acting-out. It's like diving into cold water. You just have to plunge in. "Let's act it out. Who wants to be Tom? Who wants to be Doc Robinson?" The volunteers gather at the front. You set a simple scene. "Tom and Huck stand over on that side. Doc, Injun Joe, and Muff on this side. It's midnight. Here's the graveyard. Tom and Huck enter."

The players may hesitate, but since the class show-offs were probably the first volunteers, it won't take them long to start ad-libbing. The results will probably be rather wooden or silly. The best technique, however, is just to sit at one side and let them go ahead, with perhaps an occasional word such as "Now here come Doc and Injun Joe and Muff," just to keep things moving. Suggest to the class at the outset that they must *not* interrupt the scene but let the actors play it their own way. Children love to kibbitz. But it destroys the mood, so they should be quiet — at this point — and the teacher shouldn't interrupt either, unless it's necessary to get the actors back on the track.

When the approximate end of the scene seems to have come, you can end it nicely by standing up, saying "Good," and applauding a little.

By now, others will want to try the same scene, having been thinking how they would improve on the performance while they were watching it. Some will even be waving their hands in the air as the scene ends.

After two or three sets of volunteers have acted out the scene, it's time to end things for the first day. Half an hour or forty minutes should have been enough for the whole thing.

The Second Day: Working on Characterizations

The second day, spend the half hour on characterizations, instead of acting out the whole scene. With *Tom Sawyer*, you can begin with Tom. "How does a frightened person act? How does he walk and move? How does he talk?" (Let two children demonstrate with the part when Tom and Huck first go into the graveyard.)

An impromptu scene can help. For example, if the children have trouble showing fear, say "Imagine that you and your brother are at home alone at night, and suddenly you hear footsteps in the next room. Show us how you'd move. What would you say to each other? How would your voice sound?"

Encourage the children to think about the character's state of mind, whether he is young or old, bold or shy, mean or kind, and how these things affect the voice, walk, and gestures.

A good technique is making a game of the characterizations. The children take turns pantomiming any character in the story they choose (or you assign them secretly). The class has to guess who is being impersonated.

Follow your instincts about which aspects of the characters you want to point out. In *Hansel and Gretel*, for example, the children are young and afraid. The witch is cackling and evil. (Girls love to do witches.) In *Julius Caesar*, Caesar is vain and a little pompous, and this will be reflected in his walk, gestures, and voice. As Rip Van Winkle, the actor's voice, walk, and stance must show the change from a young man to an old man. Rip's wife is a comic shrew, nagging and scolding. And encourage the children to express *their* ideas about each character.

Some children will give a comic performance of *any* part at first, from embarrassment. To show fear, they'll roll their eyes wildly and knock their knees together. As Muff Potter, the drunk, the class clown will get laughs with exaggerated reeling and staggering.

To help them, try talking over how *they* felt about each character when they were listening to the story. Isn't this the way they now want the audience to feel? In *Tom Sawyer*, Tom and Huck should seem real and every-day and human to the audience. They are not comedy parts. Injun Joe isn't funny either. He ought to frighten the audience with his cruelty. Muff Potter can be comical, but the audience ought to feel sorry for him too. Remind them that a good actor can usually wring out of the audience the emotions he wants them to feel for his character.

Some plays, of course, do call for comedy. In *The Wizard of Oz*, the cowardly lion *ought* to have quaking knees. But if the play is supposed to be serious, this is a good time to help the children distinguish between a comic and a dramatic interpretation.

One day may be enough to spend on characterizations, or you may feel like giving it two. It depends on how many difficult characters there are in the play. But don't bore the children with acting theory. After all, your classroom isn't the American Academy of Dramatic Arts. The children aren't professionals. There will be more rehearsals later. And with children, the emphasis should be on the fun of acting.

The Third Day: Acting the Scene Again

On the third (or fourth) day, act out the entire scene — from beginning to end *with no stops to discuss techniques and motivations.* Switch the cast around and do it three or four times. This should restore the flow of the scene, which was interrupted a lot during the previous session or two.

By now your play has practically cast itself, because even the shy ones (who sometimes display surprising talent) have had a chance to act out a part or two; and it's become apparent who the best actor is for each role. There are no nerve-wracking try-outs and none of the mistakes that happen when you cast a play according to who you *think* might be good.

Another advantage is that you already have a whole classful of understudies. From now on, almost any child could step into any role. (Some classes even give the same play twice with two different casts.) This is a wonderful comfort when a chickenpox epidemic breaks out the day before the play, or when the leading character begins to misbehave and you have to threaten him with loss of the part.

Most important, the scene is beginning to take on a pattern. The various actors of a role begin to imitate each other and to play the scene the same way with the same lines time after time. You may still have to encourage them a little, but the scene is starting to jell.

WRITING THE SCRIPT

How to Do It

As the scene begins to set itself into a pattern, you might jot down some of the unusually apt or funny or touching lines. Probably, however, you've become as familiar with the scene as the children have.

So after the third or fourth session, run home with your notes — or mental notes — and write a script. Yes, it really is about as easy as that. Because the children have already created most of the play just by repeating it over and over. Their words will be ringing in your head. And although you'll find yourself adding a few things (a narrator, perhaps, and some simple stage directions) and smoothing over a few places, the easiest and best thing is to use the children's language as closely as you can remember or imitate it, even if it does lack elegance.

Early the next morning run off the script on the mimeograph. The children will be surprised and delighted to recognize it as their own work.

Why Create Your Own Script?

With less advanced readers, particularly, the script is a reading lesson comparable to the primary grade experience chart, which gives the children the thrill of reading their own words in print.

Best of all, this kind of play is never too hard or too easy for your class to do. It approximates their own words and fits their language abilities — even though you may have improved slightly on the grammar. The lines are easy for them to say, unlike the stiff lines in many printed plays. The speeches are never too long to learn. The scene itself is exactly the right length and rhythm for your group.

Padding the Play

You'll probably find that the play the children have created is fairly short. You can make a longer play by acting out and writing down additional scenes from the book and just stringing them together. This depends on the ability and enthusiasm of your class.

A word of caution, though. It's better to do a short couple of scenes and stretch them into an auditorium program by adding fillers, than to try to fill forty minutes with a play that's too long for the children to do well.

There are many ways to "beef up" a play that's only approximately fifteen minutes long. Narrators can relate the gist of the book up to and after the scene. If the play is a fairy tale with a palace setting, it can open with a fanfare, a page announcing the arrival of the king and queen, and a procession of the members of the court down the aisles and onto the stage to a record of trumpet music. A court dance — two lines of boys and girls moving forward and back, bowing, and so forth — can be tucked into the middle of the play.

If the play has an early American setting, it can open and close with some period songs. You can teach a related song to the audience or lead them in some familiar songs. A child can read an appropriate poem, or a few of them can do a choral reading.

An imaginative and desperate teacher can almost always think of a way to fill in the extra time — with slides, records, or even some talented child borrowed from another class. *Anything* is better than making the play too long and spoiling it.

CASTING AND REHEARSING

Reserve the right to cast the main parts, and to choose those who did the best during the improvisations. Then throw in at least one line for every child who wants to join in, even if it's only "Make way for the King!" Some children would rather do a piece of pantomimed funny business, or be part of a chorus, a dance group, or the stage crew.

Rehearsals tend to be unstructured situations, and discipline is almost bound to fray a little. A restless child can sometimes be kept out of mischief by putting him in charge of a piece of equipment such as the record player, the curtain-pull, or a spotlight. Or you might ask another teacher to let a mischief-maker sit out a couple of rehearsals in her room. Why be a martyr at a time like this?

When children act, mumbling seems to be the toughest problem to handle. Telling the children to talk to the back of the auditorium or to shout as though they were on the playground doesn't usually work. Many children simply don't know *how* to project, consciously.

With a rote play, there's an almost foolproof method of curing mumbling: stand next to the child and speak his part one line at a time, in a good, loud, voice — well enunciated. Have the child repeat it after you, line by line. Unconsciously, he will imitate your volume and enunciation.

Unfortunately, with an improvised play, this method can kill the spontaneity. But the problem of the child who can't speak up remains. He can't feel what he's aiming for and therefore can't achieve it.

With such a child, first try reciting something not related to the play, such as a poem. If that doesn't help, then you will have to do his actual lines with him, as suggested above. But first, be sure he has had plenty of time to improvise and feel at home with his part, and be careful to imitate *the child's own acting style*. Then when he repeats the lines, he'll be imitating your projection, but in his own acting style.

The rehearsals should continue the work on characterizations you started before the script was written down. This seems to happen naturally. The children now have a script; but since they started out improvising, they usually go right on ad-libbing. This is why children doing this kind of play seldom forget a line, and why the performance is so natural. Each time they do it they're really making it up all over again. That is also why it's easy to fit in substitute players at the last minute. It's hard to rattle a cast accustomed to ad-libbing.

DOING A PRINTED PLAY

Suppose, instead of an improvised play, you choose to do a printed play. What can you do to prevent some of the stiffness that comes from memorizing?

Let the class read through the play once or twice. Then take away all the scripts. (But don't tell them you're going to, or they'll start learning by rote.) Then have them make up the lines as they remember them. They'll remember the gist — in much the same way they would act out a story you've read to them.

Above all, *don't* let the children memorize lines before they have had a chance to ad-lib the parts and think about characterizations. If they memorize the lines first, they'll be tied to them, and the performance will almost inevitably be rigid and singsong.

With a printed play — as well as with a play the children make up — the more they improvise, the better the result.

THE THREE SILLIES: NOTES

Casting: The narrator, the house-owner's group, and the twelve fools can be either male or female. To increase or decrease the cast, the narrator's part can be divided, the number of the house-owner's group and the fools can be changed, and simple lines can be doubled up, subtracted, or added.

Costumes: Modern dress is fine, or the men can wear Levi's and long-sleeved sports shirts, the women full skirts, peasant blouses, aprons, and kerchiefs.

Scenery: The peasant cottage can be painted on a piece from a big cardboard box and propped against the proscenium — or taped to a stepladder or a portable chalkboard. There must be a breakaway window, cut out, and then taped back in place so the peasant can appear to saw out the window with little effort.

Rehearsing: The twelve fools, since they have to move and ad-lib together, must rehearse this specially. They should practice silly walks, blank faces, and "dumb" voices. The overalls man and wife must be shown how to jump and fall without hurting themselves. (Have them collapse to their knees first, then catch part of their weight on their arms.)

CAST

A Narrator
A Peasant's Daughter
Her Mother
The Peasant
A House-Owner
Neighbors of the House-Owner
A Man with Overalls
The Overalls-Man's Wife
Twelve Fools

At R. a bench. At L. a peasant cottage with no windows. At center L. is a stepstool. The center R. area is empty. As the play begins, the peasant's daughter sits on the bench. The narrator stands at L.

NARRATOR: Once upon a time, there was a peasant's daughter who liked to daydream.

DAUGHTER (*in a silly, dreamy voice*): Some day I'm going to marry a handsome man, and we will have a beautiful baby boy. Maybe my little boy will grow up to be as handsome as his father. But maybe he will get sick and die. Oh, my poor little boy! (*She begins very loud, comic weeping.*) My poor little boy! (*She continues weeping.*)

(*Enter her mother.*)

MOTHER: Daughter! Daughter! What's the matter?
DAUGHTER: Some day I might have a little boy. And my little boy might die! (*Goes on weeping.*)
MOTHER: Oh, my poor little grandson! (*Mother and daughter cling together, weeping loudly.*)

(*Enter the peasant.*)

PEASANT: What's going on? What's the matter with you two?
MOTHER: Some day our daughter might have a little boy. And the little boy might die. Oh, my poor little grandson!
DAUGHTER: Oh, my poor little boy! (*Mother and daughter begin to weep again.*)
PEASANT (*bellowing*): Stop that! (*Mother and daughter break off in mid-wail and stare at him.*) You must be the two silliest people in the whole world. I'm going away, and I won't be back . . . *unless* . . . I find three people in this world who are sillier than you are!

During the narrator's next speech, the peasant puts on a cap and begins to walk toward L. Mother and daughter exit R., arms around each other, pantomiming more weeping.

NARRATOR: And so the peasant set out into the world looking for three sillies. After a few miles, he came to a small cottage.

Enter from L. a house-owner and several neighbors. The house-owner and one of the neighbors carry a big box with a lid. As they set it down, all gather around and lean in to see. The house-owner slowly lifts the lid and peers into the box. All ad-lib groans of disappointment, "Oh no," etc. The peasant watches the scene.

PEASANT: Hello, my friends. What are you doing?
HOUSE-OWNER: I'm trying to fix my house.
PEASANT: What do you mean?
FIRST NEIGHBOR: He built his house with no windows in it.
SECOND NEIGHBOR: And it's dark inside.
PEASANT: But what are you doing with that box?
THIRD NEIGHBOR: We've been up on the mountain filling this box with sunshine to carry into the house.
HOUSE-OWNER: But every time we open the lid, the sunshine has disappeared!
FOURTH NEIGHBOR: Can you help us?
PEASANT: Gladly. Do you have a saw?
HOUSE-OWNER: Yes. Here it is. (*He takes a saw from just off L. and hands it to the peasant.*)
PEASANT: Then here's how to get sunshine into your house. (*He fakes sawing out a breakaway window.*) Make a window!

House-Owner: Oh, thank you! What a wise man you are!

Peasant: And what a foolish man *you* are! At last I've found someone sillier than my wife and daughter.

Exit house-owner and neighbors. The peasant scratches his head and turns R. toward the stepstool.

Narrator: And so the peasant continued on his way.

Enter from R. a man and a woman who are carrying a pair of overalls. The peasant stands L. of the stepstool and watches the following scene.

Overalls Man: Now, let's try it again. You hold them while I jump. (*He mounts about three steps of the stool while the woman holds out the overalls for him to jump into.*)

Overalls Woman: O.K. Go ahead.

Overalls Man: A little to the left. (*She moves.*) No, a little to the right. (*She moves.*) O.K., hold it right there. One, two, THREE! (*He tries to jump into the overalls and falls in a heap, knocking down the woman at the same time. They get up and dust themselves off.*)

Overalls Man: O.K. Let's give it another try. (*He mounts the stool again. She rubs her knee and staggers a bit, but gamely holds out the overalls again.*)

Overalls Woman: O.K. Go on.

OVERALLS MAN: Steady now. One, two, THREE! (*He jumps and they both fall in a heap again. This time they get up even more slowly and both stagger and rub their heads, elbows, and backs as if dizzy and bruised.*) Well, let's give it one more try. (*He mounts the stool shakily. She holds out the overalls shakily.*) Now! (*He all but falls off the stool, and they tumble weakly to the floor. The peasant steps up to them.*)

PEASANT: Hello, my friends. What are you doing?

OVERALLS MAN (*looking up weakly*): Can't you see? I'm putting on my overalls.

PEASANT: Well, that's not the way to put on overalls.

OVERALLS MAN (*as he and wife get up and brush themselves off*): How would *you* do it?

PEASANT (*to wife*): Here. Give him those. (*To Overalls Man*) You hold them yourself. (*The wife hands them to the Overalls Man.*) Then you stand on one foot. (*The man lifts one foot.*) And you put the other foot into the overalls. (*The man does.*) Then you stand on *that* foot and put the other one into the overalls. (*The man does and breaks into a big grin.*)

OVERALLS MAN: Hey! That's easy!

OVERALLS WOMAN (*to Overalls Man*): Why didn't *you* think of that?

OVERALLS MAN: What a wise man you are!

PEASANT: And what a foolish man *you* are! (*Man and woman exit L.*) That makes two people who are sillier than my wife and daughter. If I find one more, I might as well go home.

NARRATOR: And so the peasant continued on his way.

Enter from R. twelve fools all pointing at each other and counting.

TWELVE FOOLS (*ad lib*): One, two, three . . . one, two, three, four . . . eight, nine, ten, eleven . . . (*All count at once, but no one counts higher than eleven.*)

PEASANT: Hello, my friends. What are you doing?

FOOL NUMBER ONE: Oh, good friend, help us.

FOOL NUMBER TWO: One of us drowned in the lake and we can't figure out which one it was.

PEASANT: Then how do you know one of you drowned?

FOOL NUMBER THREE: Because twelve of us went on a picnic, and now there are only eleven.

PEASANT: Are you sure?

FOOL NUMBER FOUR: Certainly. I'll show you. (*To the other fools*) Make a line. (*They line up across the stage. Fool Number Four counts, pointing to each in turn.*) One, two, three, four, five, six, seven, eight, nine, ten, eleven. (*He turns to the peasant.*) See? There are only eleven.

PEASANT (*smiling*): Maybe you made a mistake.

FOOL NUMBER FIVE: Oh, no. No matter who does the counting, we all get the same answer.

PEASANT: Show me.

The fifth fool stands before the line while the fourth takes his place.

FOOL NUMBER FIVE (*pointing to each fool in turn*):

One, two, three, four, five, six, seven, eight, nine, ten, eleven. (*To peasant*) See? There are only eleven.

PEASANT: Now let *me* try it. (*The fifth fool gets into line and the peasant counts, slowly, pointing to each one.*) One, two, three, four, five, six, seven, eight, nine, ten, eleven, twelve.

FOOL NUMBER SIX: We're all here!

FOOL NUMBER SEVEN: Nobody drowned!

FOOL NUMBER EIGHT: He counted twelve of us!

FOOL NUMBER NINE: Twelve of us!

FOOL NUMBER TEN: How did you do it?

PEASANT: It was easy. Each of you forgot to count himself!

FOOL NUMBER ELEVEN: Oh, thank you, good friend!

FOOL NUMBER TWELVE: What a wise man you are!

PEASANT: And what foolish people you are! (*As the fools file off L.*) There go *twelve* people who are sillier than my wife and daughter. The world is *full* of fools! I guess I'll just go home!

NARRATOR: So that's exactly what he did. (*Peasant goes to R. Wife and daughter step out to hug him, and they exit together R.*) And they all lived happily ever after.

HANSEL AND GRETEL: NOTES

THIS PLAY is based on the Grimms' fairy tale and on the opera *Hansel and Gretel* by Engelbert Humperdinck.

Casting: The narrator can be either male or female, and the narrator's part can be divided.

Costumes: Modern dress is fine. Boys could wear Levi's and long-sleeved sports shirts. Girls could wear ankle-length full skirts and peasant blouses.

Scenery: For the witch's house, cut a house shape from cardboard and tape it to a stepladder or portable chalkboard. Each child can make a goody from construction paper — cookie, cake, candy — and staple it to the house. Tape on two real candy sticks for Hansel and Gretel to pull off and eat. The witch's cage can be a table with cardboard "bars" on three sides. Hansel gets into the cage by crawling under the table, behind the bars. The oven can be a table covered with black paper, the door a black curtain. When Hansel and Gretel push the witch into the oven, they push her under the table, behind the curtain.

The gingerbread children can be painted on a long strip of paper attached to the backs of turned-around chairs along the back of the stage. At the beginning, it can be hidden by the back curtains, or draped. The real children hide behind it and come out when Gretel breaks the spell.

Props: The milk pitcher should be unbreakable plastic; the "milk" can be chalk ground up in water.

Music: Many songbooks contain favorite Humperdinck pieces — "Hansel Come and Dance with Me," "The Prayer," and others. Or a record of the opera can be used. Or the Humperdinck music can be eliminated. Instead of the brother-sister dance, the children can just join hands and dance in a circle. Instead of the prayer, they can pantomime praying.

CAST

A Narrator
Hansel
Gretel
Mother
Father
The Witch
The Gingerbread Children

SCENE 1

A rough cottage. On stage are two benches, a table with a pitcher and a cloth on it, several brooms, and a basket. As the curtains open, Gretel sits on one bench darning a sock, Hansel on the other with a broom across his lap. The narrator stands at L.

NARRATOR: Once upon a time a boy named Hansel and a girl named Gretel lived in the forest with their mother and their father who was a broom-maker.

HANSEL: I wish we weren't so poor, Gretel. I'm so hungry.

GRETEL: I know a secret that'll make you feel better.

HANSEL (*putting broom aside*): What secret? Tell me.

GRETEL: Say please.

HANSEL: Please.

GRETEL: Say pretty please.

HANSEL: *Pretty* please.

GRETEL: Say pretty please with sugar on it.

HANSEL: Gretel! Tell me the secret or you'll be sorry!

GRETEL: Oh, all right, grouchy. Come here. (*She beckons to Hansel. He follows her to the table.*) Look! Milk! Mother's going to make pudding with it!

HANSEL: Oh, good! (*He sticks a finger into the pitcher and licks it.*)

GRETEL (*slapping at his hand*): Don't, Hansel! Mother would be furious if she caught you. And if we don't get our work done, she'll *really* be furious.

HANSEL: I don't feel like working. There's plenty of time before Mother gets home. Teach me that dance you know.

GRETEL: Oh, all right. (*Gretel begins to sing and do the dance from the Humperdinck opera* Hansel and Gretel *as if she were showing Hansel how to do it. Hansel follows the dance awkwardly but doesn't sing. The second time through, both dance and sing.)*

As they finish, their mother enters from R.

MOTHER: What's going on here?

GRETEL: It's Hansel's fault.

HANSEL (*interrupting Gretel*): It's Gretel's fault.

MOTHER: Quiet! (*She picks up Gretel's sock.*) You didn't finish your sock, Gretel. (*She looks at the brooms.*) And Hansel, you haven't made enough brooms. Oh, you bad children! (*She pushes them and they stumble against the table. The pitcher of milk spills.*) Look what you did! Just wait till your father gets home!

HANSEL: The pudding! Now there won't be any pudding!

MOTHER: Whose fault is that? Here. (*She hands Hansel a basket.*) Go to the woods and get some strawberries for supper. And come back with a full basket, or it will be too bad for you! (*She pushes them both and they trudge off L.*)

MOTHER: Oh, what will I do? (*She wipes up the milk with a cloth.*) Nothing to eat. Not a crumb for my poor hungry children! (*She begins to weep.*)

Enter the father from R., very cheerful.

FATHER: I'm home! What's for supper?

MOTHER: Nothing! And plenty of it!

FATHER (*Setting down a basket and taking out a loaf*

of bread, some apples, etc.): That's what *you* think! Look at this!

MOTHER (*amazed*): Where did you get all that food?

FATHER: There was a crowd in town today, and I sold all my brooms. Wait till Hansel and Gretel see this. (*He calls.*) Hansel! Gretel! Come and see what I have! (*Pauses.*) Where are they?

MOTHER: I sent them to the woods for strawberries.

FATHER: You sent them to the woods alone? But don't you know that's where the Evil One lives?

MOTHER: What do you mean?

FATHER: There's a wicked witch in that forest. She captures children and bakes them in her magic oven until they turn into gingerbread.

MOTHER: Then what does she do?

FATHER: She *eats* them!

MOTHER: Oh, how terrible! Hurry! We must find them!

They run toward L. as curtains close.

SCENE 2

The forest. As the curtains open, Hansel and Gretel enter from L. Their basket is empty.

GRETEL: Oh, Hansel. You ate all the strawberries. How can we go home with an empty basket?

HANSEL: Me? You ate half of them yourself!

GRETEL: I couldn't help it. I was hungry. (*She starts to cry.*)

HANSEL: Don't cry, Gretel. I was the one that started

eating them. Maybe we can fill the basket again.

GRETEL: No, we can't, Hansel. It's getting dark. We'd better go home right now, or we'll get lost.

HANSEL: I think we *are* lost, Gretel.

GRETEL: What?

HANSEL: I said, I think we *are* lost. I've been looking for the path and I can't find it.

GRETEL (*looking around*): Oh, Hansel. What'll we do?

HANSEL: We can't be far from home. I think if we just lie down and go to sleep, Mother and Father will find us in the morning.

GRETEL: I guess that's all we can do. (*They sit down on the stage.*) Hansel, I'm scared.

HANSEL: Don't be scared, Gretel. If we say our prayers, the angels will watch over us.

Hansel and Gretel kneel, fold their hands, and sing the prayer from the opera Hansel and Gretel *by Humperdinck. Then they lie down.*

GRETEL: We'll be all right now. Good night, Hansel.

HANSEL: Good night.

Curtain

SCENE 3

The next morning. The scene is the same as before, but now the witch's house has appeared at R. A big oven is near the center. At L. is a cage. Across the back is a row of gingerbread boys and girls. As the curtains open, Hansel and Gretel sit up, stretch, and yawn.

GRETEL: Oh look, Hansel. What a beautiful house!
HANSEL: I didn't see it last night, did you?
GRETEL: No, but it looks good enough to eat. (*She gets up and runs to the house. Hansel follows. She pulls off a candy stick and takes a bite.*) Oh, Hansel! This is good. Try some.
HANSEL (*pulling off and biting into another candy stick*): Mmmmmmmmmmmmmm.
WITCH (*from off R.*): Nibble, nibble, little mouse. Who is nibbling on my house?

Hansel and Gretel look at each other, startled. They start to back away from the house just as the witch enters carrying a rope and a stick.

WITCH: What nice children! Did you come to visit me? (*She throws the rope around Hansel.*)
HANSEL: Help! Help! Let me go! (*He struggles free and runs toward L. with Gretel right behind him.*)
WITCH (*holding up the stick and chanting*): Hocus pocus, hocus pell. Now I cast my magic spell! (*Hansel and Gretel freeze in midstep.*) Now, come here you delicious-looking children. (*Hansel and Gretel walk back to her in a trance. The witch pokes her finger into Hansel's stomach.*) You're too skinny. I think I'll fatten you up for my Christmas dinner. (*She leads Hansel to the cage and puts him inside.*) That's a good boy. You just stay there. (*To*

Gretel) And you, my dear, you can help me with my work. (*She exits R.*)

GRETEL (*standing stiff, still under the spell*): Oh, Hansel, what'll we do?

HANSEL: Be quiet, Gretel. Keep an eye on her and do what she tells you. Maybe we'll think of a way to break the spell and get away.

The witch re-enters carrying a basket of food. She feeds Hansel a carrot.

WITCH: Eat up, my dear. You'll soon fatten up. (*She turns to Gretel.*) Meanwhile, I'll take the spell off this one. As long as her brother is in the cage, she will obey me. (*She holds up the stick and chants over Gretel.*) Hocus pocus, hocus pell. I take away the magic spell!

Gretel moves her arms and legs in relief. The witch lays down the stick.

WITCH: Now, my dear, go check to see how hot the oven is. (*She turns to feed Hansel another carrot. While her back is turned, Gretel grabs the magic stick and waves it toward Hansel.*)

GRETEL: Hocus pocus, hocus pell. I take away the magic spell!

WITCH (*turning to Gretel*): What did you say?

GRETEL (*hiding the stick behind her back*): I said I I don't know how to check the oven.

WITCH: You silly goose! You just stick your head in to see if it's hot enough.

GRETEL: But I don't know how.
WITCH: Stupid child. Watch me. (*She goes to the oven, opens it, and puts in her head. Meanwhile Hansel slips out of his cage and comes up behind her. Hansel and Gretel give her a push. She falls in and Gretel slams the door.*)
GRETEL: The witch is dead!
HANSEL: The witch is dead!

> *Hansel and Gretel take hands and dance around in a circle chanting "The witch is dead! The witch is dead!" Behind them, the gingerbread children begin to moan and groan.*

GRETEL: The gingerbread children!
HANSEL: Are they alive?
GINGERBREAD BOY: Help! Help!
GINGERBREAD GIRL: We're under the witch's spell!
GRETEL (*holding up the witch's stick*): Hocus pocus, hocus pell. I take away the magic spell!

> *The gingerbread children ad-lib "Hurray" and run to Hansel and Gretel who begin to sing and do the brother-sister dance from Scene 1. The gingerbread children join in, taking random partners, dancing and singing wildly and joyfully. As the song ends, enter the mother and father from L.*

FATHER: Hansel!
MOTHER: Gretel!
FATHER: We've been looking for you all night.

MOTHER: Are you all right? (*All hug each other as the narrator, at L., speaks.*)

NARRATOR: And so the witch was dead, the enchanted children were free, and Hansel and Gretel and their parents all lived happily ever after.

All, including the mother and father, begin to dance and sing again as the curtains slowly close.

TOM SAWYER: NOTES

The end of Scene 1 and Scene 2 were written by Class 5-2, P.S. 190-M, New York, 1961. It was our first effort, and we made the mistake of choosing a scene with a small and all male cast. The schoolroom scene has been added as a partial correction.

Casting: The narrator can be either male or female and the narrator's part can be divided. There can be any number of school children.

Costumes: Modern dress is fine. The boys can wear Levi's and long-sleeved sports shirts. The girls can wear ankle-length full skirts, long-sleeved blouses, and long hair ribbons.

Props: The knife should be rubber or cardboard. A "dead cat" can be made from an old fur hat.

Scenery: The schoolroom is just rows of lunchroom benches. For the graveyard, a tree can be painted on cardboard and taped to the proscenium. Two or three bushes and some gravestones can be painted on construction paper and taped over the backs of turned-around chairs. (Kindergarten-size chairs are good for gravestones.)

Rehearsing: Injun Joe must practice a fake stabbing (between Doc Robinson's upstage arm and side) and Doc must practice falling so as not to be hurt (first to his knees, then full length, catching his weight partially with one arm).

CAST

A Narrator
Tom Sawyer
Huckleberry Finn
Injun Joe
Doc Robinson
Muff Potter
Becky Thatcher
A Group of Girls
A Male School Teacher
School Children

Narrator: Class 5-2 has enjoyed many books and stories this year. One of our favorites is *The Adventures of Tom Sawyer* by Mark Twain. The scene we will do today is called "Tragedy in the Graveyard." The time is 100 years ago. The place: a one-room country schoolhouse. Everyone is working hard—everyone, that is, but Huck Finn.

SCENE 1

A one-room schoolhouse. As the curtains open, a teacher stands at R, facing boys and girls (separated) on rows of benches. Enter at R. Huck Finn carrying a dead cat. He leans against the proscenium. During his speech, the teacher and children do not move.

HUCK: Look at 'em sittin' there on a nice day like this. I got thrown out of school a long time ago, and it was fine with me. I wouldn't be here now, but I want to show this (*Holds up cat.*) to Tom Sawyer. (*He leans back and watches the rest of the scene.*)

TEACHER: All right, children. We'll sing one song. What will it be? (*Becky raises her hand.*) Becky Thatcher?

BECKY: Let's sing "School Days."

TEACHER: All right. "School Days." (*He leads the group in the song.*) That was very good, children. School is dismissed!

The children get up and noisily leave the stage from both sides, ad-libbing after-school remarks as the curtains close. Becky, Tom, Huck, and a few girls remain before the curtain.

BECKY: Tom? Where are you going?

TOM: I got to talk to Huck, Becky. See you later.

GIRLS (*in sing-song*): Beck-y likes To-om! Beck-y likes To-om!

BECKY (*turning*): I do not! You take that back! (*She chases them off stage.*)

Tom (*approaching Huck*): What you got there, Huck?

Huck: Dead cat.

Tom: What's a dead cat good for?

Huck: Get rid of warts, that's what.

Tom: Yeah? How d'you work a dead cat for warts?

Huck: Well, you got to take it to the graveyard at midnight when they've just buried a bad man. At midnight, the devil comes to get his soul, and when he comes, you throw the cat after him and say, "Dead man follow devil, cat follow dead man, warts follow cat."

Tom: And that gets rid of 'em?

Huck: Gets rid of warts every time.

Tom: Gee.

Huck: Wanta come with me tonight? They just buried old Hoss Williams, and I reckon he's about the baddest man ever was.

Tom: O.K., Huck. You whistle for me tonight, and I'll sneak out and meet you.

Huck: O.K. But don't let your Aunt Polly hear you! (*They exit together R.*)

Narrator (*at L.*): Just before midnight, Tom climbed out a window and ran to meet Huck. Soon they arrived at the graveyard.

SCENE 2

The graveyard. There are tombstones and a tree. As the curtains open, enter from R. Tom and Huck on tiptoe, carrying dead cat.

Huck: Now, we got to sit here by this tree and wait for the devil to come. (*They sit.*)

Tom: It's scary here. I'm glad there's a full moon tonight.

Huck: Yeah.

Tom: How bad was Hoss Williams — that bad man's buried here?

Huck: Awful bad. He killed a man, and they hung him.

Tom: Do you reckon the dead can hear us talkin'?

Huck: I reckon so.

Tom: I wisht I'd said *Mr.* Williams. But everyone called him Hoss.

Huck: Shush, Tom! You see that light movin' through the trees yonder?

Tom: Yeah, I see it. That the devil comin'?

Huck: Must be. That's devil fire, sure. We got to be real quiet, so's he won't hear us. And stay out of sight!

Voices are heard off L.

Tom: Wait! That ain't the devil. That's young Doc Robinson's voice.

Huck: You're right, Tom. And that's Injun Joe with him.

Tom: And old Muff Potter. But what're they doin' here at this time of night?

Huck: I don't know, but shush up. They mustn't know we're here! (*They crouch back against the tree.*)

Enter from L. Doc, Injun Joe carrying a lan-

tern, and Muff Potter carrying a spade. Muff is drunk.

INJUN JOE (*setting down the lantern*): Here's the grave. Hurry and dig it up!

MUFF: D'ya really think old Hoss had valuables buried with him?

DOC: Sure. He had a watch and a ring, and maybe some money in his pockets.

MUFF: Well, let's hurry, then. (*He bends over to dig. Joe gives him a push, and he falls unconscious. Joe takes Muff's knife and grabs Doc by the throat.*)

JOE: D'you remember one time I came to your door hungry and you had me put in jail for begging? Well, I never forgot that. Now I got you! (*He stabs Doc, then puts the knife in Muff's hand.*)

MUFF (*coming to*): I must've passed out. I . . . Why, look at Doc! He's dead!

JOE: I tried to stop you, but I was too late.

MUFF (*seeing the knife in his hand*): You mean *I* did it?

JOE: Like I said, I tried to stop you, but before I could, you'd killed him.

MUFF: Oh, no! I knew I should have stopped drinking, but I never hurt anyone before. (*Drops to his knees.*) Oh, Injun Joe, you won't tell I did it, will you?

JOE: No, Muff, you been good to me. I won't tell.

MUFF: Oh, thank you, Injun Joe. Thank you.

JOE: We'd better get out of here!

They scramble to pick up the spade and lantern, then run off, leaving Doc lying on stage. Tom and Huck approach Doc and look at his body.

Tom: Oh, Huck, it's awful! Muff Potter didn't kill him. Injun Joe did! What'll we do?

Huck: Nothing. If we ever told on Injun Joe, he'd kill us, sure.

Tom: Then we got to swear never to tell. We'll write it down.

Huck: We'll never tell till we die!

Tom: And we'll sign it in *blood!*

Huck: Yeah. In blood!

Tom (*scared*): Hucky, let's go home.

Huck: Let's run!

They exit, running, leaving the cat behind. Enter narrator at L.

Narrator: Muff Potter was so scared that he confessed killing Doc. When Muff was put on trial, Tom's conscience bothered him so much he went to court and told everyone he had seen Injun Joe kill Doc. Injun Joe jumped out the courtroom window and ran; but he gave Tom and Huck and Becky plenty of trouble before he was caught.

Class 5–2 hopes *you* will read *The Adventures of Tom Sawyer,* too.

THE WIZARD OF OZ: NOTES

This play is adapted from a play by classes 5–1 and 5–2, P.S. 154-X, New York, 1962–63.

Casting: The narrator and the Munchkins can be either male or female. There can be any number of Munchkins, and the narrator's part can be divided.

Costumes: Modern dress. The good witches are in white, the wicked witch in black. The wizard wears a modern suit, but at first carries a huge, ugly mask that hides him. The scarecrow wears old Levi's fringed at the bottom, a plaid shirt or sweatshirt, and a straw hat. The tin woodman's body is a big silver-painted cardboard box with armholes. His arms and legs can be wrapped in foil. He wears a pointed silver cap. His ax can be silver-painted cardboard. The lion needs a pajama-like brown suit. A bouncy tail can be made by winding wire around a broom handle, covering it with crepe paper, then pulling the handle out. Yarn over the head makes a mane, and a tuft of yarn at the end of the tail adds a touch. Paint on whiskers with eye-liner. Arched eyebrows are amusing. Toto needs a costume like the lion's with a plain tail, close-fitting cap, and ears shaped from wire. The Munchkins traditionally wear blue. If this isn't possible, cut the word *blue* from the script.

Scenery: Scene 2, the land of the Munchkins, should have flowers and greenery. They have to appear in front of the curtain quickly, so some artificial flowers and greenery can be carried on in small boxes. The yellow brick road can be edged with real bricks painted yellow, or yellow-painted wood blocks, or strips of yellow paper taped to the stage. There can be a few more little boxes of artificial flowers along the yellow brick road.

Props: The "brains" can be a bean bag. The "heart" can be cut out of cardboard and covered with red foil, with tape on the back, ready to be stuck onto the woodman's chest. The "courage" can be a bottle of red-colored water. The witch's spyglass can be a painted cardboard tube from a roll of paper towels.

Music: The suggested music is from the film *The Wizard of Oz* and the songs are recorded. The music can be substituted for as follows: Eliminate "Over the Rainbow"; replace "Ding Dong, the Witch Is Dead" with a general shout of "hurrah"; replace the first "We're off to See the Wizard" with waving, thank-you's, good-bye's, and good-luck's from Dorothy and the Munchkins. Where Dorothy, the scarecrow, the woodman, and the lion sing snatches of "We're off to See the Wizard," they can skip along chanting the words "We're off to see the wizard, the wonderful wizard of Oz" instead.

CAST

A NARRATOR
AUNT EM
UNCLE HENRY
DOROTHY
TOTO
THE GOOD WITCH OF THE NORTH
A CROWD OF MUNCHKINS
THE SCARECROW
THE TIN WOODMAN
THE COWARDLY LION
THE GUARDIAN OF THE GATES
THE WIZARD
THE WICKED WITCH OF THE WEST
THE GOOD WITCH OF THE SOUTH

SCENE 1

Kansas. Before the curtain. The narrator is at L.

NARRATOR: Once there was a little girl named Dorothy. (*Enter Dorothy from R. At center, she faces the audience.*) Dorothy lived with her Aunt Em and her Uncle Henry. (*Enter Em and Henry from L. They stand next to Dorothy, center.*) And her little dog, Toto. (*Enter Toto from R. He also stands next to Dorothy.*) Dorothy and Aunt Em and Uncle Henry and Toto lived on a farm on the prairie in Kansas. And sometimes Dorothy was not very happy. (*Em and Henry move L., fold arms, and watch.*)

DOROTHY (*kneeling with Toto*): Oh, Toto, everything here in Kansas is gray. (*She points out over audience.*) The dirt is gray and the grass is gray and the house is gray. Sometimes I dream about a place where the grass is green and the birds are blue and the flowers are all different colors. (*She sings "Over the Rainbow" from the film,* The Wizard of Oz.)

NARRATOR: Dorothy didn't know it, but her dream was just about to come true.

EM (*walking to edge of stage and pointing over audience*): Look, Henry! There's a storm coming!

HENRY (*walking up next to Em*): Hey! That's no storm! That's a cyclone!

EM: Then we'd better get into the cyclone cellar! (*She runs down steps at L., or off L.*)

HENRY: Come on, Dorothy. It's a cyclone! Hurry up! (*He exits L.*)

Dorothy starts to follow, then stops and turns.

DOROTHY: Wait! Where's Toto? Toto! Where are you? (*Toto runs to R.*) Toto! Come here! (*Dorothy*

runs after Toto and tries to pull him toward L.)
NARRATOR: But before they could get to the cellar, the cyclone picked up the house with Dorothy and Toto in it, and carried it away.

Dorothy and Toto whirl around and around across the stage and off L.

SCENE 2

The Land of the Munchkins. In front of the curtain there are a few branches with colorful flowers. Two feet wearing silver shoes stick out from under the curtain. The narrator stands at L.

NARRATOR: After many hours, Dorothy's house landed with a bump; and Dorothy and Toto came outside to see where they were.

DOROTHY (*as she and Toto enter from L.*): Well, I know one thing, Toto. This isn't Kansas. Look at those flowers! What a beautiful place!

Enter from R. the Good Witch of the North, followed by the Munchkins, entering from both sides.

GOOD WITCH OF NORTH: Welcome to Oz, and thank you for killing the Wicked Witch of the East.

DOROTHY: Who, me? I didn't kill anyone.

GOOD WITCH OF NORTH: Well, your house did, anyway. It landed right on the wicked witch. See? There are her feet sticking out from under it. (*She points.*)

DOROTHY: Oh! That's awful!

GOOD WITCH OF NORTH: No, no! It's wonderful. She made slaves of these blue Munchkins. Now she's dead and the Munchkins are free!

MUNCHKIN NUMBER ONE: We're free!

MUNCHKIN NUMBER TWO: We're free!

The Munchkins sing "Ding Dong, the Witch Is Dead" from the film The Wizard of Oz.

DOROTHY: Well, I'm glad I could help. But who are you?

GOOD WITCH OF NORTH: I'm the Good Witch of the North. Who are you?

DOROTHY: I'm Dorothy and this is Toto. We're from Kansas, and we'd better get back. How do you get to Kansas from here?

GOOD WITCH OF NORTH: I'm afraid I don't know. There are terrible deserts all around the Land of Oz.

DOROTHY: But can't anyone help me get home again?

GOOD WITCH OF NORTH: Well, there *is* someone who might.

DOROTHY: Who?

GOOD WITCH OF NORTH: The wizard. He's the wisest man in Oz. He can do anything.

DOROTHY: That's wonderful. How can I find him?

GOOD WITCH OF NORTH: Well, first you'd better put on the wicked witch's silver shoes for luck. (*As Dorothy takes the shoes and puts them on, the curtains open to reveal the yellow brick road.*) And now, you just follow the yellow brick road.

DOROTHY: Follow the yellow brick road?
GOOD WITCH OF NORTH AND MUNCHKINS: Follow the yellow brick road.

The Munchkins sing the verse of "We're Off to See the Wizard" picking up the rhythm from the preceding lines. Dorothy sings the words "We're Off to See the Wizard, the Wonderful Wizard of Oz" then all finish the song together as Dorothy skips along the yellow brick road which winds across the stage. As the song ends and the curtains close, all wave and exit both sides.

SCENE 3

The yellow brick road. As the curtains open, a scarecrow stands up center, arms out and dangling loosely from his elbows, knock-kneed, head down.

Enter from L. Dorothy and Toto. Dorothy skips and sings a few lines of "We're Off to See the Wizard." At center, almost in front of the scarecrow, Dorothy sits down without seeing him.

DOROTHY: Let's sit down a minute, Toto. I'm tired. (*She wipes her face with a handkerchief.*)
SCARECROW (*lifting his head*): Nice day, isn't it?
DOROTHY (*looking to right and left but seeing no*

one): I thought I heard someone say, "Nice day, isn't it?" But I must have imagined it.

SCARECROW: No you didn't. It was me.

DOROTHY (*whirls toward the scarecrow, turns back to audience, and turns to the scarecrow again*): You?

SCARECROW: Certainly. There's nobody here but you and your dog and me. The dog can't talk, and it wasn't you, so it must have been me.

DOROTHY: I didn't know scarecrows could talk.

SCARECROW: Oh, yes, certainly, certainly.

DOROTHY: Well, then, how do you do? I'm Dorothy and this is Toto.

SCARECROW: And I'm the scarecrow, and now that we're friends, I wish you'd do me a favor.

DOROTHY: What?

SCARECROW: Take me down off this pole. I've been up here for two days!

DOROTHY: Oh, sure. (*She "lifts" the scarecrow and he staggers about loose-jointedly, getting his balance.*)

SCARECROW: Oh, that's much better.

DOROTHY: Good. Now will you do *me* a favor?

SCARECROW: What's that?

DOROTHY: Tell me, am I going the right way to find the wizard?

SCARECROW: Oh, dear, I'm afraid I can't tell you *anything*. My head's full of straw. I don't have any brains. What's a wizard?

DOROTHY: He's the wisest man in Oz. I'm going to ask him to send me home to Kansas.

SCARECROW: Would the wizard give me some brains?
DOROTHY: I don't know, but why don't you come with me? You can't be any worse off than you are now.
SCARECROW: That's true. Let's go!

> *They sing a few bars of "We're Off to See the Wizard" as they skip toward R. At R., the tin woodman edges stiffly onstage, ax raised over his head.*

WOODMAN (*groaning*): Oooh! Oooh!
DOROTHY: What's that?
SCARECROW: I don't know.
WOODMAN: Oooh! Oooh!
DOROTHY: It's that tin woodman! (*She goes up to the woodman.*) Are you groaning?
WOODMAN (*squeakily*): Yes.
DOROTHY: What's the matter?
WOODMAN: I'm rusty. Oil my joints!

> *Dorothy picks up an oil can just off R. and oils the woodman's elbows and shoulders. He brings his arms slowly down and puts down his ax. She oils his neck and he moves his head from side to side. She oils his knees and he takes a few stiff steps, tottering comically. He should walk a bit stiff-jointedly throughout the play.*

DOROTHY: Is that better?
WOODMAN: Oh, yes! I've been standing there since I got caught in the rain last year. But now I can walk again.

SCARECROW: Then why don't you walk to the wizard with us?

WOODMAN: Who's the wizard?

SCARECROW: The wisest man in Oz. Dorothy is going to ask him to send her back to Kansas, and I'm going to ask him for some brains.

WOODMAN: Do you think he'd give me a heart?

SCARECROW: Wouldn't you rather have brains? If you don't have brains, you won't know what to do with a heart!

WOODMAN: But brains will never make you happy, and happiness is the best thing in the world.

DOROTHY: Well, come on, and maybe we'll all get what we want.

They all sing a few lines of "We're Off to See the Wizard" as they skip back toward L. At L. the lion jumps out with a huge roar.

LION: Roar! Roar!

TOTO (*running at the lion*): Bow wow! Bow wow!

LION (*turning on Toto*): Roar! Roar!

DOROTHY (*slapping the lion on the nose*): Don't you dare bite Toto, you bad lion! Shame on you, picking on a little dog. You're nothing but a big coward!

LION: You're right. I *am* a coward. (*He begins to sob loudly.*)

DOROTHY: I'm sorry. I didn't mean to make you cry.

LION (*drying his tears with the tip of his tail*): No, you're right. I'm supposed to be King of the Beasts, but I really don't have any courage at all!

DOROTHY: Then why don't you come with us?

LION: Why?

DOROTHY: We're going to see the wizard. The scarecrow is going to ask him for some brains. And the tin woodman wants a heart. And I want to go back to Kansas. Maybe you should ask for some courage!

LION: Well, I think I will!

They sing "We're Off to See the Wizard" and skip off R. as the curtains close.

SCENE 4

The palace of the wizard. Before the curtain. As the scene begins, the narrator is at L.

NARRATOR: After many miles and many adventures, Dorothy, Toto, the scarecrow, the tin woodman, and the lion reach the palace of the wizard, where they meet the Guardian of the Gates.

Enter the Guardian of the Gates from R., followed by Dorothy and the others.

GUARDIAN: Follow me! (*He leads them to center, faces the curtains, and announces.*) Oh, great wizard, here are five people . . . (*He looks the group over and starts again.*) Here are five who wish to speak with you. (*He steps backward and exits L.*)

The wizard steps out from between the curtains. He holds the huge mask of an ugly head in front of himself.

WIZARD (*in a big, booming voice*): I am the wizard, great and terrible. Who are you?

Dorothy: I am Dorothy, small and meek. Oh, great wizard, we need your help.

Scarecrow: I want some brains.

Woodman: I want a heart.

Lion (*nervously*): And I want some . . . some . . . (*He hides his face in Dorothy's shoulder.*)

Wizard (*loudly*): Speak up!

Lion (*jumping with fright*): . . . some courage!

Dorothy: And Toto and I want to go back to Kansas. Can you help us?

Wizard: I can.

Dorothy: Oh, thank you! (*Scarecrow, woodman, lion, and Dorothy join hands and dance around for joy.*)

Wizard: But I won't!

All stop dancing

Dorothy: You won't? You won't help us?

Wizard: Not until *you* do something for *me*.

Dorothy: But what can we do for you?

Wizard: You killed the Wicked Witch of the East.

Dorothy: But I didn't mean to. My house fell on her.

Wizard: Never mind. Now you must kill the Wicked Witch of the West.

Dorothy: Oh, but I couldn't do that! I never killed anything in my life — on purpose.

Wizard: Go kill the Wicked Witch of the West. Then come back and I will help you.

Dorothy: But . . .

Wizard: Go! (*He backs off between the curtains, still holding the mask in front of himself.*)

COWARDLY LION (*crying*): What are we going to do? Now I'll never get my courage.
SCARECROW: And I'll never get my brains.
WOODMAN: And I'll never get my heart.
DOROTHY: And I'll never get back to Kansas.
TOTO: Woof!

They wander sadly toward R.

DOROTHY: I could *never* kill anybody — even a wicked witch! Besides, I don't even know where she lives.

They pause at R. as the Wicked Witch of the West enters at L. She carries a spyglass.

WICKED WITCH (*chuckling wickedly as she watches them through the spyglass*): He-he-he, ha-ha! You don't know where I am, Dorothy; but I know where *you* are. I see that stupid scarecrow. I see that tinhorn woodman. I see that silly lion and that yappy dog . . . and I can see you and your silver shoes. Those silver shoes have a magic power. I want those shoes, and I'm going to get them! (*Standing on her left foot*) Ep-pe, pep-pe, kak-ke! (*Standing on right foot*) Hil-lo, hol-lo, hel-lo. (*Standing on both feet*) Ziz-zy, zuz-zy, zuk. (*She waves her hand toward the group.*) Dorothy, come here!

Dorothy and the others whirl helplessly toward the witch, ad-libbing "Oh, ah," etc. Meanwhile the curtains open.

57

WITCH: Now you are my prisoners. You (*pointing at the lion, scarecrow, woodman, and Toto*) — into the dungeon! (*She waves them off L.*) And you (*to Dorothy*) take this bucket and scrub my floor! (*She takes a bucket from just off L., getting rid of the spyglass at the same time, and gives the bucket to Dorothy. Dorothy pulls out a scrub brush and kneels to scrub the floor.*) And now I'll take those silver shoes! (*The witch pulls one of Dorothy's shoes off her foot.*)

DOROTHY: Oh, you mean old witch! Those are my lucky shoes. Give it back!

WITCH: Don't be silly! I'll get the other one too. And then you and your friends will die!

As the witch grabs for the other shoe, Dorothy throws the bucket of "water" at her.

DOROTHY: Oh, you *are* wicked!

WITCH: No! Water melts me! Help! You killed me! I'm melting! I'm melting! (*Her voice fades out and she crumples to the floor, pulling her cape up over her head so that she looks like just a heap of black clothing.*)

DOROTHY: She's dead! (*She touches the witch.*) She's dead! We're free! (*She runs to L. and pulls on the lion and the others.*) We're free! Look! The witch is dead! (*She takes her silver shoe and puts it back on.*)

SCARECROW: Now the wizard *has* to help us!

All sing "Ding Dong, the Witch Is Dead."
Curtain

SCENE 5

The palace of the wizard a little later. Before the curtain. The narrator stands at L.

NARRATOR: Dorothy and her friends went back to the palace of the wizard, sure he would help them, now that the Wicked Witch of the West was dead.

During the narrator's speech, the Guardian of the Gates enters at R., followed by Dorothy and the others. They stop at center and the Guardian faces the curtains.

GUARDIAN: Great wizard, the five have returned! (*He exits L.*)

WIZARD (*entering behind the huge mask*): Oh, it's you again. What do you want?

DOROTHY: The Wicked Witch is dead, and you said you would help us.

SCARECROW: You said you'd give me some brains.

WOODMAN: And you said you'd give me a heart.

LION: And you said you'd give me some c-c-c-courage.

DOROTHY: And you said you'd send me back to Kansas.

WIZARD (*clearing his throat nervously*): Yes. Fine. Come back in a few days and I'll let you know.

DOROTHY (*angrily*): That's not fair! You said you'd help us! You've had plenty of time to think it over!

SCARECROW: That's right.

TIN WOODMAN AND LION: Yeah!

TOTO: Woof! Woof! (*He jumps and knocks the mask*

59

aside, revealing the "wizard" as a very timid-looking man.)

DOROTHY: Who are *you?*

WIZARD: Don't hit me! Don't hit me!

DOROTHY: Nobody's going to hit you. But who are you? Where's the wizard?

WIZARD (*fearfully*): I'm the wizard.

DOROTHY, SCARECROW, WOODMAN, AND LION: You?

WIZARD: But I'm not really a wizard. I've been pretending for years. I'm just a big fake. I'm afraid I can't help you at all.

DOROTHY: But then why did you ask us to kill the Wicked Witch of the West?

WIZARD: Because she knew who I was, and she could have hurt me. Besides, I didn't think you could do it, and then you wouldn't come back here again, asking for miracles.

DOROTHY: But who are you really?

WIZARD: I used to do a balloon act, and one day the wind carried my balloon away and I landed here. When the people saw me coming out of the sky, they thought I was a great wizard. And I let them think so.

DOROTHY: But we were counting on you. What will we do?

WIZARD: Well, maybe I can help your friends, anyway.

DOROTHY: How?

WIZARD: Watch. Scarecrow, come here. (*The curtains open to reveal a table with various odds and ends on it.*) You want brains. (*He picks up a small bag.*) Here's some bran. That should be just as good.

SCARECROW: Oh, yes, thank you. (*He puts the bag under his hat.*) Oh, yes! I can think better already!

WIZARD: And woodman, you want a heart. I just happen to have one here. (*He picks up a big red heart and fastens it to the woodman's chest.*)

WOODMAN: Oh, thank you. I've never been so happy in my life!

WIZARD: And lion, you want some courage. Here is a bottle of courage I've been saving for years. (*He picks up a bottle of red liquid. The lion drinks it.*)

LION: Oh, thank you. I feel so brave! (*He shadow boxes comically.*)

DOROTHY: But what about me? Can you help me get back to Kansas?

WIZARD: I'm afraid not. After all, I'm not a real wizard.

DOROTHY (*beginning to cry*): But I want to go home!

Enter from L. the Good Witch of the South.

GOOD WITCH OF SOUTH: Maybe I can help you, Dorothy.

DOROTHY: Oh! Who are you?

GOOD WITCH OF SOUTH: I'm the Good Witch of the South. All of us here in Oz are grateful to you for killing the Wicked Witches. My sister, the Good Witch of the North helped you find the wizard. Maybe I can help you get back to Kansas.

Dorothy: Oh, how?

Good Witch of South: It's the silver shoes. They're magic. That's why the Wicked Witch wanted them.

Dorothy: What should I do?

Good Witch of South: Just close your eyes and say three times, "I want to go back to Kansas." The shoes will carry you home.

Dorothy: Then I'll do it right away. And thank you!

Scarecrow (*starting to weep*): Are you going away, Dorothy?

Lion (*wiping his eyes with his tail*): Are you really going, Dorothy?

Dorothy: Oh, dear. I hate to leave you. But I really do want to go home.

Lion: That's all right, Dorothy. (*He sobs.*)

Scarecrow: That's all right, Dorothy. (*He sobs, then looks at the tin woodman who has not said anything.*) What's the matter with you? Aren't you sorry Dorothy is leaving?

Woodman: I can't cry. I'll rust! (*He starts to cry.*) Oh, dear!

Dorothy (*picking up an oil can from the wizard's table*): Poor woodman. (*She oils his neck.*) Is that better?

Woodman: Yes. But who'll oil me if you go away?

Dorothy: You'll all have to take good care of each other now. (*She hugs each one.*) Good-bye, woodman. Good-bye, lion. Good-bye, scarecrow. We'll miss you very much. (*She puts her hands on*

Toto's shoulders and as the curtains close slowly, she closes her eyes and says the spell.) I want to go back to Kansas. I want to go back to Kansas. I want to go back to Kansas. (*She and Toto whirl around and around and come out between the curtains just as they close. Aunt Em enters L.*)

EM: Dorothy! Where have you been?

DOROTHY (*running to her and hugging her*): I've been in the Land of Oz. And oh, Aunt Em, I'm so glad I'm home again!

RIP VAN WINKLE: NOTES

Casting: Narrator, child with yo-yo, and villagers can be either male or female. The narrator's part can be divided, and villagers' lines can be added, subtracted, or doubled up.

Costumes: Modern dress is fine. To approximate period dress, the men can stuff pants into knee socks and wear rough shirts. The women can wear white caps (a crepe paper circle gathered into a cap), white cape-like collars crossed over the front to the waist, long skirts, and big aprons. The ghosts can wear old skirts divided to make blousy pants, knee socks, rosettes at the knee, and either full-sleeved white blouses with squared Pilgrim collars and big hats with ribbons and plumes, or striped T-shirts and pirate-type kerchiefs on their heads. They should wear sashes and swords or knives at the waist, and shoes with foil-covered cardboard buckles.

Props: Steins can be foil-covered coffee mugs. The keg can be a spouted picnic jug covered with brown crepe paper. Bowling pins can be cut from styrofoam so they don't crash when they fall. The bowling ball can be any rubber ball.

Scenery: Scene 2 can be a few bushes and trees painted on construction paper and pinned to the back curtains or taped over the backs of turned-around chairs.

Sound effects: Rumble the bottom keys on a piano or beat a cymbal with a muffled stick for thunder.

Rehearsing: The villagers must coordinate movements and ad-libbed lines. The ghosts must bowl between the narrator's lines so he is not drowned out by thunder.

CAST

A NARRATOR
RIP VAN WINKLE
A CHILD
DAME VAN WINKLE
THE GUIDE
A COMPANY OF GHOSTLY DUTCHMEN
TWO PUBLIC SPEAKERS
A CROWD OF VILLAGERS
JUDITH GARDINIER
RIP, JUNIOR
RIP III (*small child*)
SIX WOMEN
AN OLD WOMAN
PETER VANDERDONK

SCENE 1

Before the curtain. A bench is against the proscenium at R. A narrator stands at L.

NARRATOR: Many years ago, near the Catskill Mountains of New York, there lived a simple, good-natured fellow by the name of Rip Van Winkle.

During the next part of the narrator's speech, Rip enters from R. shuffling lazily. From L. comes a child with a yo-yo hanging by its string, crying. Rip winds the string. The child skips happily off R.

NARRATOR: Rip was a good neighbor. He was kind to animals. He played with the children and fixed their broken toys. (*Pause to let Rip and child finish.*) Yes, Rip was a wonderful fellow. In fact, he had only one fault: He couldn't bear to work.

Rip sits on the bench, folds his arms, yawns, leans against the proscenium, and goes to sleep.

NARRATOR: And Rip's wife also had one fault: She couldn't bear to leave Rip alone.

Enter from behind the proscenium Rip is leaning against, Dame Van Winkle, carrying a broom.

DAME VAN WINKLE (*very loud and scolding*): Rip! Rip! (*She shakes his shoulder roughly.*) Get up from that bench. I have to sweep!

Rip looks up sleepily, gets up, and stands aside obediently. Dame Van Winkle sweeps under the bench, then sweeps in a semicircle until she runs into Rip. He tries to sidestep her, but she sidesteps the same way. He moves left, she moves left; he moves right, she moves right; he moves left again; she

67

moves left again. Finally she stops, one hand on her hip.

DAME VAN WINKLE: Rip! You nuisance! Sit down! You're in the way!

Rip sits down and goes back to sleep. Dame Van Winkle gives one or two swipes with the broom, then shakes Rip again.

DAME VAN WINKLE: Rip! You lazy lout! Get up! I need the dustpan!

Rip gets up slowly and steps behind the proscenium while Dame Van Winkle sweeps things into an imaginary pile. Rip returns with the dustpan, hands it to her, and stands behind her while she bends down to sweep up the pile. She moves slowly backward until she bumps into Rip.

DAME VAN WINKLE (*turning to Rip*): Rip! You pest! I told you to sit down. How can I work with you standing there?

Rip sits down and goes back to sleep. Dame Van Winkle puts the pan out of sight offstage. She comes back with the broom and stands over Rip, arms akimbo. Impatiently, she shakes him.

DAME VAN WINKLE: Rip! You oaf! Get up! Why aren't you working in the field? This farm is falling apart!

RIP (*standing slowly*): This is a poor piece of land,

my dear. Nothing grows right, no matter what I do.

DAME VAN WINKLE: No matter what you do! What have you been doing? Yesterday you slept all day!

RIP: Why, yesterday I was going to plow. But just as I started out, it began to rain!

DAME VAN WINKLE: Rip! You'd rather starve on a penny than work for a dollar! I think you're the laziest man that ever lived! (*Rip shrugs and looks at the ceiling.*) Now get out of this house. I don't want you under foot. *I* have work to do, even if you don't! Go on! (*She sweeps at his heels with her broom.*) Shoo! And don't go fishing! Do some work for a change!

Rip shuffles off across stage and exits L. Dame Van Winkle looks after him, harumphs as he exits, then stalks off R.

SCENE 2

A mountainside. As the curtains open, the narrator stands at L.

Enter Rip from L., a gun on his shoulder. He trudges slowly across toward stage R.

NARRATOR: Poor Rip. The only way he could escape was to take a gun and wander through the woods. One day he found he had climbed to one of the highest parts of the Catskill Mountains.

RIP: I've been climbing all day. I'm worn out. (*He sits and leans against R. proscenium.*)

NARRATOR: Rip sat for a long time, gazing at the

Hudson River far below. (*Rip looks down over the apron.*) Before he knew it, it was evening.

RIP (*sitting up suddenly, worried*): Look how late it is! (*He stands up and picks up his gun.*) It'll be dark before I get home. What will my wife say?

Enter up L. the guide, an old man dressed in the fashion of the 1500's, carrying a keg.

GUIDE (*calling*): Rip Van Winkle! Rip Van Winkle!

RIP (*to audience*): He seems to know me. It must be one of my neighbors. (*To guide*) Hello, friend! Can I give you a hand with that? (*He hurries to the guide. The guide hands the keg to Rip and points silently toward R.*) I'll be glad to help.

During the narrator's next lines, Rip and the guide move toward R. as if climbing laboriously. Part way across, Rip stops as if exhausted and the guide takes the keg. Almost at R., the guide gives it back to Rip, as if it is very heavy. They toil slowly off R.

Narrative with pantomime follows.

NARRATOR: Rip wondered why the old man was so silent, but he seemed so strange that Rip was afraid and asked no questions. Together, they carried the keg up the mountain without exchanging a word.

Thunder is heard

NARRATOR: A sound like thunder came from high on the mountain, and Rip wondered if it was going to rain.

Rip and the guide exit R., then quickly cross behind the upstage curtain to re-enter at L. If there is no upstage curtain, they can re-enter from R. As Rip and the guide leave stage, a band of men, also dressed in the fashion of the 1500's, enter at L. One carries ninepins and a ball in a basket and sets up the pins at L. Two bring a bench. Each one brings his own mug or stein, plus two for the guide and Rip. They set them on the bench, leaving room for the keg. They step back and begin to take turns silently bowling a ball at the pins. Throughout the scene the men continue to bowl in silence, paying no attention at all to Rip. Thunder sounds each time the ball is rolled, so the bowling must be timed to fall between the narrator's lines.

NARRATOR: At last, Rip and the old man came to a hidden hollow, (*Enter at L. Rip and the guide*) and there was a group of strange-looking men playing at ninepins. They were all dressed like the Dutchmen of 200 years before. And though they were playing a game, no one smiled or said a word. The only sound was a sound like thunder when they bowled. The old man set down the keg (*The guide puts the keg on the bench.*) and motioned Rip to serve the men.

The guide points to Rip, then to the keg, the steins, and the men. The guide joins the others at bowling, and Rip fills the steins and hands them to the men.

Before long, Rip began to feel more at ease. He even drank what the men were drinking.

Rip fills a stein and swallows it hastily.

It tasted good.

Rip sneaks another stein of liquor.

It was *very* good.

Rip takes another.

Before long, Rip felt so drowsy that he just lay down and went to sleep.

Rip lurches toward down R., curls up on the floor, and goes to sleep.
Curtain

SCENE 3

Twenty years later, the same spot. As the curtains open, Rip is in the same position as at the end of Scene 2, but now he wears rags, a long white beard and a white wig. A rusty, battered gun lies beside him. The narrator stands at L. The rest of the stage is bare.

NARRATOR: When Rip woke up, he was in the place where he had first seen the strange old man.

Rip yawns, stretches, and gets up very stiffly.

Rip: Am I stiff! And no wonder! I must have slept out here all night. (*He takes a few stiff steps.*) I think I've caught a little rheumatism. My wife will be furious. (*He picks up his gun.*) My gun! It's all rusty! What happened to it? (*He scratches his head. Then he looks up as if an idea has come to him.*) Now I remember! Those men! I'll bet they took my gun and left me this old one! Just wait till I find those thieves! I'll soon make them give me back my gun! (*He begins to walk toward L., then stops.*) It's gone! The path we took is gone! I can't find it! (*He shakes his head.*) I don't know what I was drinking, but whatever it was, it scrambled my brains. I guess there's nothing I can do but go home. (*He limps stiffly off L., shaking his head as he goes.*) What will my wife say? What will she say?

Curtain

SCENE 4

Before the curtain. The narrator stands at L.

Narrator: Poor Rip turned his steps toward home, afraid to tell his wife he had fallen asleep in the woods and lost his gun. Little did he know what a surprise was in store for him.

The town square. As the curtains open, the first speaker is standing on a box, surrounded by a group of villagers.

First Speaker (*waving a small American flag*): He's

the best man for the office! (*The villagers ad-lib cheers and boos.*) Cast your vote for the most honest man on the ballot! (*More cheers and boos.*)

The second speaker jumps up on the box. As he starts to speak, Rip shuffles on from L.

SECOND SPEAKER (*also waving a small American flag*): No! No! He's all wrong. The only man to vote for is . . .

FIRST WOMAN (*pointing at Rip*): Look! Look at that!

The crowd turns to stare and point and ad-lib giggles, ooh's, and ah's. The speaker trails off.

RIP (*to audience*): I don't understand it. This is my town. (*He points to the top of the upstage curtain.*) There are the Catskill Mountains. (*He points down over the apron.*) There's the Hudson River. I *know* this is my town. But all the houses are different, and I don't recognize anyone!

Rip shuffles a step or two toward the crowd, and they back away. Girls cover their mouths and look shocked. Men rub their chins as they look at Rip. Rip finally reaches up to rub his own chin and discovers the beard.

Why, I've grown a beard a foot long! What on earth has happened to me?

The second speaker jumps down from the

box, elbows through the crowd, and steps up to Rip.

SECOND SPEAKER: Who are you voting for, old man? Are you a Federal or a Democrat?
RIP: I don't know.

The first speaker pushes up to the front.

FIRST SPEAKER: What do you mean by coming to an election with a gun? Who are you, anyway?
RIP: Me? I'm a native of this town — a loyal subject of His Majesty the King of England!
CROWD (*ad-lib*): A spy! A spy! He's a spy!
FIRST SPEAKER (*to crowd*): Quiet! (*To Rip*) Why did you come here? Who are you looking for?
RIP: Well, I'm just looking for someone I know. I'm looking for my old friends.
SECOND SPEAKER: Who are they? Name them!
RIP: Nicholas Vedder. Where's old Nicholas?
SECOND WOMAN: Nicholas Vedder's been dead for eighteen years!
RIP: Where's Brom Dutcher?
THIRD WOMAN: Brom was killed in the war.
RIP: Well, then, where's Van Brummel, the schoolmaster?
FOURTH WOMAN: Don't you know? Van Brummel was a general in the army and now he's in Congress.
RIP (*covering his ears and moaning*): What are you talking about? A war? Congress? What are these things? And how can Nicholas Vedder be dead?

I saw him yesterday! (*He clasps his hands to plead.*) Don't you know Rip Van Winkle?

FIFTH WOMAN: That's Rip Van Winkle over there. (*She points to a young man slouching at one side.*)

SIXTH WOMAN: But you still haven't told us who *you* are.

RIP (*near tears*): I don't know. Yesterday I was myself, and today I'm somebody else!

The villagers begin to nudge each other and twirl their fingers at their temples to indicate craziness. A little boy pulls at his mother.

BOY (RIP III): Mommy, that man is crazy!

HIS MOTHER (JUDITH GARDINIER): Hush, little Rip! That's not nice.

Rip recognizes the woman. He steps toward her.

RIP: Excuse me, what is your name?

JUDITH: Judith Gardinier.

RIP: What is your father's name?

JUDITH: Rip Van Winkle was his name, the same as my brother there (*The young man, Rip, Jr., moves over next to her.*) and my son. (*She puts her hand on Rip III's shoulder.*) But the poor man left home twenty years ago and no one ever saw him again.

RIP: And where is your mother?

JUDITH: My mother died last year.

RIP: Judith! Rip! I'm your father! Once I was young Rip Van Winkle! Now I'm old Rip Van Winkle!

(*To the crowd*) Does nobody know poor Rip Van Winkle?

An old woman hobbles up to him and leans on a cane, peering into his face.

OLD WOMAN: Sure enough! It *is* Rip Van Winkle. Welcome home, neighbor. Where have you been these twenty long years?

Rip begins to speak, then fades off into pantomime as the narrator begins to speak.

RIP: Well, one day I was up in the mountains . . .

NARRATOR: Rip's story was soon told. After all, to Rip, the twenty years were like one night. At first, many people refused to believe him. But then, old Peter Vanderdonk stepped forward.

PETER VANDERDONK: Rip's story is true. The Catskill Mountains have always been haunted. Henry Hudson explored this river two hundred years ago; and every twenty years, he comes back with the ghosts of his crew. My own father once saw them in a mountain hollow. They were wearing old-fashioned Dutch clothes, and playing the old game of ninepins. I myself have heard them bowling. On a summer evening, it sounds like thunder.

NARRATOR: So Rip had slept for twenty years — right through the Revolutionary War. When he went to sleep, he was a subject of the King of England. When he woke up, he was a citizen of the United States.

Rip puts one arm around Rip, Jr., and one

around Judith. The family walk slowly and happily toward R. The crowd stands frozen in place.

NARRATOR: But Rip didn't care about politics. The only government that ever made *him* unhappy was the government of his wife! He soon found many of his old friends; and he made new friends too. He went to live with his daughter and his son. And he was a happy man to the end of his days.

Rip and family exit as the curtains close.

JULIUS CAESAR: NOTES

THIS PLAY is adapted from Shakespeare and from a similar play by Class 6–1, P.S. 49-X, New York, 1965–66.

Casting: Narrator, members of the crowd, the first and last two Roman women, the soothsayer, and Lucia can be either male or female. (The latter two are male in Shakespeare.) To increase the cast, add to the members of the crowd and divide the narrator's part. To decrease the cast, cut the first two Roman women and Decius and Trebonius. Give Decius' and Trebonius' lines to others.

Costumes: Modern dress is fine. To approximate Roman costumes of Caesar's time, the women can wear *stolas* or tunics (plain dresses) hanging straight to the instep with a tie at the waist, any length sleeve. In public, they would wear *pallas* (cloaks) draped over the left arm, over the head, around the right arm, and the end slung over the left shoulder again. The dress and cloak can be any color, particularly soft yellow, blue, or green. Off-red shades (called purple by the Romans) were reserved for the high-born at this time.

The men would wear *togas*, white for the common citizens, with reddish (purple) borders for the high-born — in this case the conspirators, Mark Anthony, and Caesar. Caesar might have an entire toga of red. A sheet makes a good toga. It must reach to the instep. It drapes over the left arm, around the back, *under* the right arm, then is slung over the left arm again and down the back. Underneath, the Romans wore tunics. A T-shirt will do. The high-born would have a red stripe (a ribbon is fine) over the right shoulder from front to back. The soothsayer should wear a dark cloak.

Props: The daggers should be rubber or cardboard.

Scenery: In Scene 2, Brutus' garden can be a couple of bushes painted on construction paper and taped over the backs of turned-around chairs. In Scene 3, Caesar's house can be two or three lunchroom benches draped with fancy cloth and with a few cushions thrown around.

Rehearsing: The Roman crowd should have a separate rehearsal, because they move and ad-lib together; and since much of the action takes place in the presence of the crowd, they have to practice looking at and reacting to the right characters. The stabbing of Caesar must be rehearsed so that the conspirators stab him and step back without blocking each other or Caesar. Caesar's fall is broken by grabbing Brutus' shoulders, so he should not be hurt in the fall.

Reading *Julius Caesar* to the class: At this age, Shakespeare will be easiest to digest if you tell them the story and read some selected famous lines as the story unfolds. Encourage discussion of the characters, and go over lines from the original Shakespeare play that characterize Caesar, Cicero, Cassius, Brutus, Anthony, Calpurnia, and Portia. Be sure the children are familiar with the characters and their names, so that they don't confuse them.

CAST

A NARRATOR
FIVE ROMAN WOMEN
JULIUS CAESAR
MARK ANTHONY
BRUTUS ⎤
CASSIUS |
CASCA |
CICERO   } CAESAR'S MURDERERS
DECIUS |
TREBONIUS ⎦
CALPURNIA, CAESAR'S WIFE
PORTIA, BRUTUS' WIFE
A SOOTHSAYER
LUCIA, BRUTUS' SERVANT
A CROWD OF ROMAN CITIZENS

SCENE 1

A Roman street. Before the curtain. As the scene begins, the narrator stands at L.

NARRATOR: The time: Thirty-five years before Christ

was born. The place: Rome. (*Pause*) For hundreds of years the Roman people have had a republican government with *elected* officials. But now, a Roman general has become very powerful, and some people are afraid he wants to be king. (*Pause*) His name: Julius Caesar. (*Exit the narrator.*)

Shouts are heard off R. as the Roman crowd ad-libs "Hurrah!" etc. Enter from L. two Roman women.

FIRST ROMAN WOMAN: What's going on? What's all the shouting?

SECOND ROMAN WOMAN: Everyone's waiting to see Caesar.

Enter from R. Caesar, Mark Anthony, Brutus, Cassius, Cicero, Casca, Decius, Trebonius, Calpurnia, and Portia, followed by a soothsayer and the Roman crowd, some onstage, some below stage. Some throw flowers at Caesar. All ad-lib "Hurrah! Caesar!" and applaud. The soothsayer steps up to Caesar.

SOOTHSAYER (*loudly and urgently*): Caesar! Caesar!

(*The crowd quiets.*)

CAESAR: Well, old woman. What's my fortune?

SOOTHSAYER: Beware, Caesar! Beware the Ides of March!

CAESAR: The Ides of March? That's weeks from now,

old woman. Go away. Don't bother me with your bad dreams. (*The soothsayer steps back into the crowd. Caesar and others exit L., except Brutus and Cassius, who holds Brutus' arm to keep him from going.*)

Cassius: You don't look well lately, Brutus.

Brutus: I've got a lot on my mind, Cassius.

Cassius: I don't like to see a great man like you so long-faced.

Brutus: I know you, Cassius. What are you up to?

Cassius: Nothing, Brutus. I just wish you knew how much the people love you.

(*Off L. the crowd ad-libs "Hurrah!"*)

Brutus: Listen to that. The people love Caesar, not me. I'm afraid they're going to make him king.

Cassius (*with emphasis*): You're *afraid*? Then you don't like the idea. I thought you were Caesar's friend. You used to be his *best* friend.

Brutus: I love Caesar, but he's gotten so powerful. I'm worried. But what's on *your* mind, Cassius?

Cassius: Listen, Brutus. I have a story to tell you. One time, Caesar dared me to swim across the Tiber with him in a storm. But about halfway across I heard him yelling, "Help! I'm going under!" I saved his life.

Brutus: Yes. I know about that.

Cassius: And once when we were in Spain he came down with a fever and cried like a girl.

Brutus: What's your point?

Cassius: He's no better than we are. But now he

thinks he's a god and we have to bow to him. I think we should do something about him.

BRUTUS (*sadly*): I understand, Cassius. I know some of you are talking about killing him. I suppose you want me in on it. (*Pause*) Killing my friend, though ... it would almost kill *me*. Still, I'll think it over.

CASSIUS (*grasping Brutus by the hand*): That's good enough for now, Brutus.

Off L. the crowd ad-libs, "Hurrah!" again.

BRUTUS: Here he comes again.

Enter Caesar and the crowd. As Caesar passes Cassius, he stares at him and continues to stare back over his shoulder as he goes by.

CAESAR: Anthony! Mark Anthony!
ANTHONY: Caesar?
CAESAR: I like fat, happy people around me. Look at that Cassius. He has a lean and hungry look. I don't like it.
ANTHONY: Don't be afraid of Cassius.
CAESAR: I'm not. I'm not afraid of anyone.
ANTHONY: Wait, Caesar! (*One of the crowd puts a box before Caesar.*) Step up here.
CAESAR: What's this?

Anthony takes Caesar by the elbow and helps him up on the box. A servant hands a coronet to Anthony. The crowd ad-libs

"Ooh, aah." Anthony holds up his hand for silence.

ANTHONY (*loudly*): Noble Caesar. Take this crown.

CAESAR (*sternly pushing aside the coronet with the back of his hand*): No, Anthony. I don't want a crown.

To Caesar's surprise, the crowd cheers and applauds.

ANTHONY (*putting up hand for silence again*): Rome needs a strong leader. Take the crown!

CAESAR (*hesitating, then pushing aside the crown, but less firmly than before*): No, Anthony. Rome has never had a king.

Again the crowd cheers and applauds.

CAESAR (*to Calpurnia*): Listen to the crowd cheering when I say no to the crown. Maybe the people are against me.

CALPURNIA: Oh, no, Caesar. The people love you.

ANTHONY: Caesar, I beg you. Take the crown.

Caesar hesitates and looks over the crowd, at Calpurnia, then at Anthony. Slowly he pushes the crown aside.

CAESAR: I will not take the crown.

Again the crowd cheers and applauds.

CAESAR (*grabbing Casca's arm and clutching at his own throat*): Casca! Cut my throat!

CASCA: Caesar! What are you saying?

CAESAR: The people hate me! Quick! Kill me!
CASCA (*horrified*): No, Caesar!

As Casca speaks, Caesar faints. Three Roman women rush from the crowd and kneel beside him.

THIRD ROMAN WOMAN: Caesar!
FOURTH ROMAN WOMAN: Oh, Caesar!
FIFTH ROMAN WOMAN: Poor Caesar! (*The women wipe his forehead, pat his hand, etc.*)
CICERO (*to Casca*): First the people cheer when Caesar turns down the crown. Then, when he faints, they rush to help him. Maybe the people really *do* love Caesar!
CASCA: Oh, those silly women! They'd act like that even if Caesar had stabbed their mothers.
CICERO: Sometimes even *I* feel sorry for Caesar. He has the falling sickness, you know.
CASCA: Did he faint because he was sick? Or because he knew the crowd didn't want him to take the crown?
CICERO: Hmm. Caesar said no to the crown; but of course he really wanted it. Some day he may take the crown even if the people don't want a king.

Caesar has revived, and Anthony and Calpurnia help him to his feet. The crowd ad-libs murmurs of sympathy. All exit R. except Cassius and Brutus.

BRUTUS: We'll talk tomorrow, Cassius. Good-bye for now. (*He exits L.*)

Cassius (*to audience*): I'm worried about Brutus. He's afraid of Caesar's power . . . but he loves him too. When the time comes to kill Caesar, will he be with us, or against us? (*He begins to exit R.*) Well, I have a lot of work to do. (*He exits.*)

SCENE 2

Brutus' garden before dawn. As the curtains open, the narrator stands at R.

Narrator: Several weeks passed. Then one night Brutus couldn't sleep.

Enter Brutus from L.

Brutus (*looking at the sky*): What time is it? It's too dark tonight to tell. (*Calls off L.*) Lucia!

Enter Lucia.

Lucia: Sir?
Brutus: Bring me a candle.
Lucia: Yes, sir. (*She exits L.*)
Brutus (*to audience*): I've been awake all night wondering what to do. Tomorrow I'm sure the senators are going to offer Caesar the crown — and this time, he'll take it. The power will go to his head, and he'll make slaves of the Roman people. Caesar is like a snake's egg. If we let him hatch, he'll be dangerous. I think we'd better kill him in the shell.

Enter Lucia with a candle.

LUCIA: Here is a candle, sir.
BRUTUS: Thank you, Lucia. (*Pause*) Lucia, what day is this?
LUCIA: The fifteenth of March, sir, when the sun rises.
BRUTUS: The fifteenth . . . the Ides of March. It's the day the old soothsayer warned Caesar about. Then, this will be the day to do it.

Knocking is heard off R.

BRUTUS: Go to the gate, Lucia. Someone is knocking.

Lucia goes to R., then steps back to allow Casca, Cicero, Cassius, Decius, and Trebonius to enter.

CASSIUS: I know it's late, Brutus. I hope we didn't wake you. But something has to be done. We've heard that tomorrow the senators are going to give Caesar the crown.
BRUTUS: I know. I've been awake all night; and you don't need to say more. I've decided to join you.
CASSIUS (*shaking Brutus' hand*): You won't be sorry.
DECIUS: Then let's decide what we're going to do. Should we kill only Caesar?
CASSIUS: Mark Anthony and Caesar are good friends. Anthony could make trouble for us. Let's kill them both.
BRUTUS: Don't be so bloody, Cassius. We're not butchers. Anyway, Anthony is just a playboy. He's harmless. Let's leave him alone.

CASSIUS: I don't know. You know how much he loves Caesar.
TREBONIUS: Anthony only loves himself. He's never been serious about anything in his life. I'm not worried about Anthony.

A clock strikes three.

BRUTUS: Wait! The clock is striking!
CASSIUS: It's three o'clock.
TREBONIUS: We'd better leave.
CASSIUS: Wait! There's one thing I'm worried about. Will Caesar come to the Senate today? Do you remember the day the soothsayer told him, "Beware the Ides of March?"
TREBONIUS: The Ides! That's today!
CASSIUS: And Caesar's gotten superstitious lately. What if he decides to stay at home?
DECIUS: I can usually talk Caesar into anything. I'll go to his house and bring him myself.
CASSIUS: Then it's all settled. We'll meet at the Senate. It's the last time we'll see Caesar alive.

Exit R. all but Brutus, ad-libbing "Good night." As they leave, enter Portia from L.

PORTIA: Brutus?
BRUTUS: Portia! What are you doing up at this hour?
PORTIA: I could ask you the same thing. What's wrong?
BRUTUS: I haven't been feeling well.
PORTIA: If you were sick you'd stay *in* bed, not get

out of it in the middle of the night. I think the sickness is in your mind.

BRUTUS: It's nothing.

PORTIA: Who were those men who came just now? What do they want?

BRUTUS: Just some business.

PORTIA: Brutus, I'm your wife. I want to know what's going on.

BRUTUS (*taking her arm*): Then come inside. I'll tell you all about it.

Exit L. Brutus and Portia. Curtain.

SCENE 3

Caesar's house just after dawn. As the curtains open, Caesar stands at center.

CAESAR: What an awful night. Three times my wife screamed in her sleep.

Enter Calpurnia from R.

CALPURNIA. Why are you up so early, Caesar? Are you going out? I don't want you to leave the house today.

CAESAR: Don't be silly, Calpurnia. I have to go to the Senate. I'm making a speech today.

CALPURNIA: Caesar, that dream I had was a death warning from the gods.

CAESAR: Should I think about dying every time you have a bad dream?

CALPURNIA: Then stay home for me. Tell everyone it's because *I'm* afraid. Please.

Caesar (*laughing*): Oh, well, all right. If it will make you happy, I'll stay at home today.

Enter Decius from L.

Decius: Hail, Caesar. I've come to take you to the Senate.

Caesar: Then you're just in time to take a message for me. I won't be there today.

Decius: But why?

Caesar: To please my wife. Calpurnia had a bad dream last night.

Calpurnia: I dreamed I saw Caesar's statue, and there were a hundred spouts running out of it, and out of every spout ran blood. And a lot of people were smiling and washing their hands in the blood.

Decius: But that's not a bad dream. That's a *good* dream.

Calpurnia: How can that be a good dream, Decius?

Decius: Blood running from Caesar's statue and Romans washing their hands in it — that shows that Rome is getting new life blood since Caesar began to rule.

Caesar: You know, I think you're right!

Decius: I *know* I'm right. I happen to know that this is going to be a very good day for you, Caesar.

Caesar: How do you know that? Are you a fortune-teller?

Decius: No, but I do know a secret. I shouldn't tell you. It's supposed to be a surprise. But the Senate is going to give you the crown today.

CAESAR: Then it *was* a good dream! Come on, Decius. I don't want to be late.

Exit Decius and Caesar L. Calpurnia looks after them, then exits slowly R., head down, as curtain closes.

SCENE 4

The Capitol, half an hour later. As the curtains open, the soothsayer stands at center. Enter Caesar from L., with Decius. At the same time, a crowd enters from both sides, including the conspirators. The crowd and conspirators stay back, leaving Caesar and the soothsayer alone in the center.

CAESAR (*taking the soothsayer by the arm*): I remember you, old woman. You see? I'm still alive, and the Ides of March have come!

SOOTHSAYER: But not gone! (*The soothsayer steps back into the crowd.*)

CAESAR (*now alone in the center, looking out over the crowd*): So many Romans here today, and all of them want to speak to me. Who should I listen to first?

The conspirators and other members of the crowd call out Caesar's name, interrupting each other.

CICERO: Caesar!
TREBONIUS: Caesar!
CASCA: Caesar!

CAESAR (*holding up hands for silence. When crowd is quiet, he speaks*): Casca, what do you have to say?

CASCA: Caesar . . . (*takes out dagger*) My hands speak for me! (*He steps forward and stabs Caesar.*)

Throughout, and until the end of the scene, the crowd ad-libs murmurs of excitement and fear: "What's going on?" "They're killing Caesar!" "Caesar is dead!" etc., but subdued enough that the voices of Caesar and the conspirators are heard above them.

One by one, Cassius, Cicero, Trebonius, and Decius step forward and stab Caesar with daggers that were hidden in their robes. As each stabs, he steps back to let the next one stab so that the murder is almost graceful and formal. Caesar staggers and clutches his wounds but still stands. Last, Brutus steps up and stabs him.

CAESAR (*aghast — This is his best friend.*): You, too, Brutus? Then I die! (*He pitches forward, grabs Brutus by the shoulders for a second, then falls.*)

CASSIUS (*holding up his dagger*): Liberty! Freedom!

CONSPIRATORS (*ad-lib*): Liberty! Freedom!

Only Brutus remains silent, staring at the body.

Curtain

EPILOGUE

Curtains closed. The narrator stands at L.

NARRATOR: The murderers thought they had won. But Mark Anthony, Caesar's friend, the man they had decided not to kill, wanted revenge. At Caesar's funeral, Anthony made a clever and bitter speech that turned the Roman people against the murderers. Civil war broke out. On one side: the army of the murderers, Cassius and Brutus. On the other side: the army of Mark Anthony. Anthony's army won, and Cassius and Brutus committed suicide.

When the war ended, Caesar's nephew took the crown Caesar had turned down. This nephew of Julius Caesar was called Caesar Augustus. He became a great and powerful ruler, and so the House of Julius Caesar began to rule the Roman Empire.